JAN 1 5

JR. GRAPHIC AMERICAN LEGENDS

JOHN HENRY

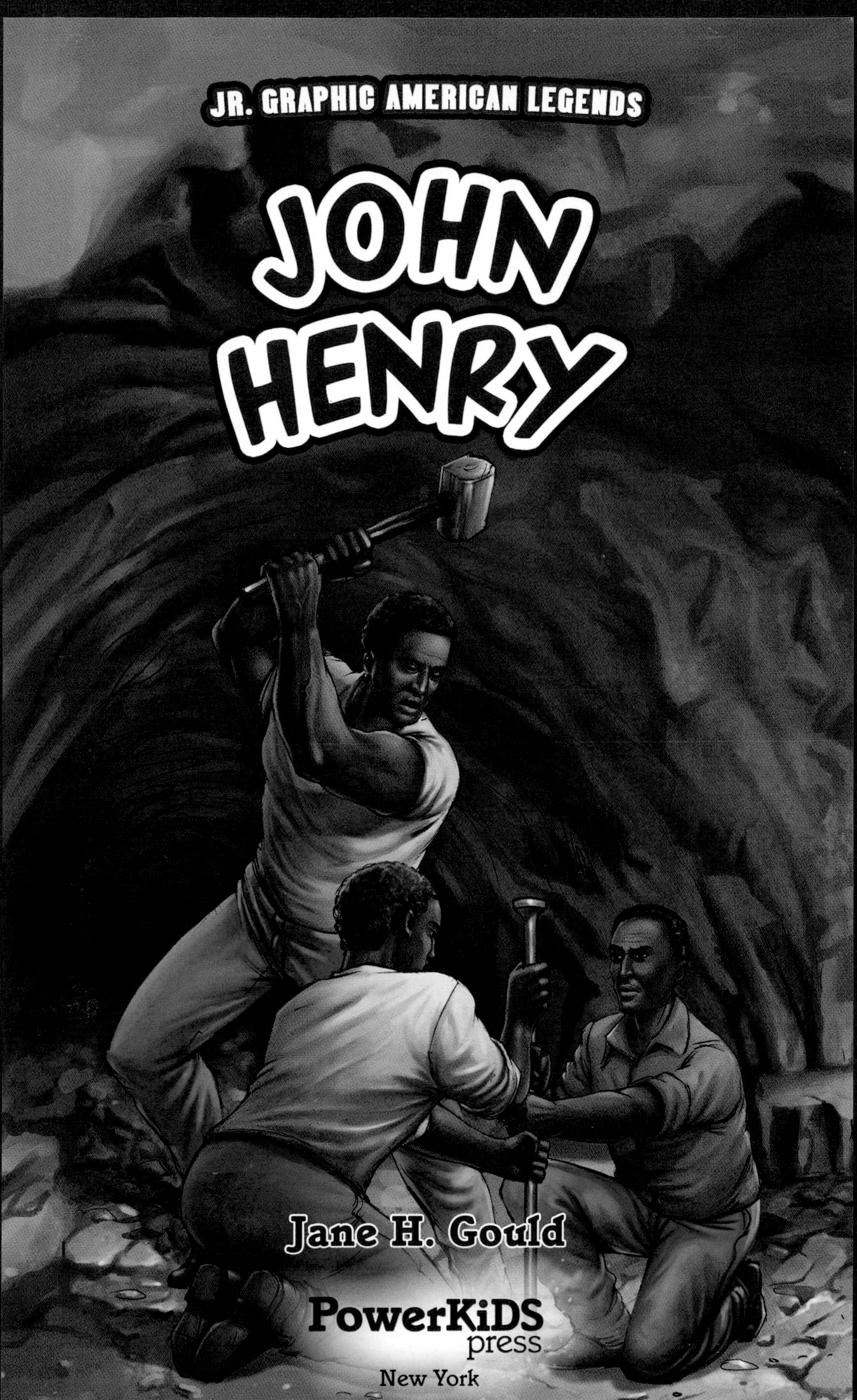

Jane H. Gould

PowerKiDS press
New York

Published in 2015 by The Rosen Publishing Group, Inc.
29 East 21st Street, New York, NY 10010

First Edition

Editor: Joanne Randolph
Book Design: Contentra Technologies
Illustrations: Contentra Technologies

Library of Congress Cataloging-in-Publication Data

Gould, Jane H.
John Henry / by Jane H. Gould. — First edition.
    pages cm. — (Jr. graphic American legends)
 ISBN 978-1-4777-7197-6 (library binding) — ISBN 978-1-4777-7198-3 (pbk.) —
ISBN 978-1-4777-7199-0 (6-pack)
1. John Henry (Legendary character)—Legends. [1. John Henry (Legendary
character)—Legends. 2. African Americans—Folklore. 3. Folklore—United
States.] 1. Title.
 PZ8.1.G68Joh 2015
 398.2—dc23
 [E]
                                    2013049380

Manufactured in the United States of America
CPSIA Compliance Information: Batch #WS14PK2: For Further Information contact Rosen Publishing, New York,
New York at 1-800-237-9932

Contents

Introduction

After the **Civil War**, building railroads to link the East Coast and the West Coast became a major goal of the nation. Sometimes, it was necessary to dig tunnels through mountains so that trains could pass from one region to another. At first, railroad companies used men for this job, but soon they wanted to replace the men with a machine, called a **steam drill**, that could dig faster. John Henry was one of the men who dug those tunnels. He showed that a man could be better than a machine.

Main Characters

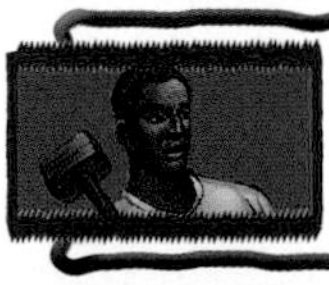

John Henry A strong man who helped dig railway tunnels in the 1870s.

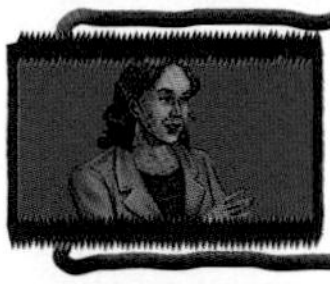

Ms. Becker A fifth-grade teacher.

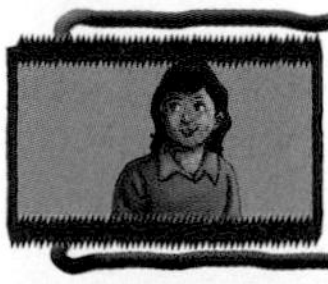

Haley A fifth-grade student.

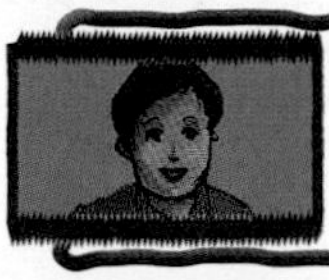

Kyle A fifth-grade student.

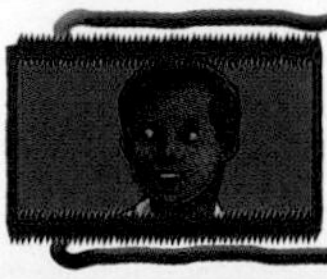

Reggie A fifth-grade student.

JOHN HENRY

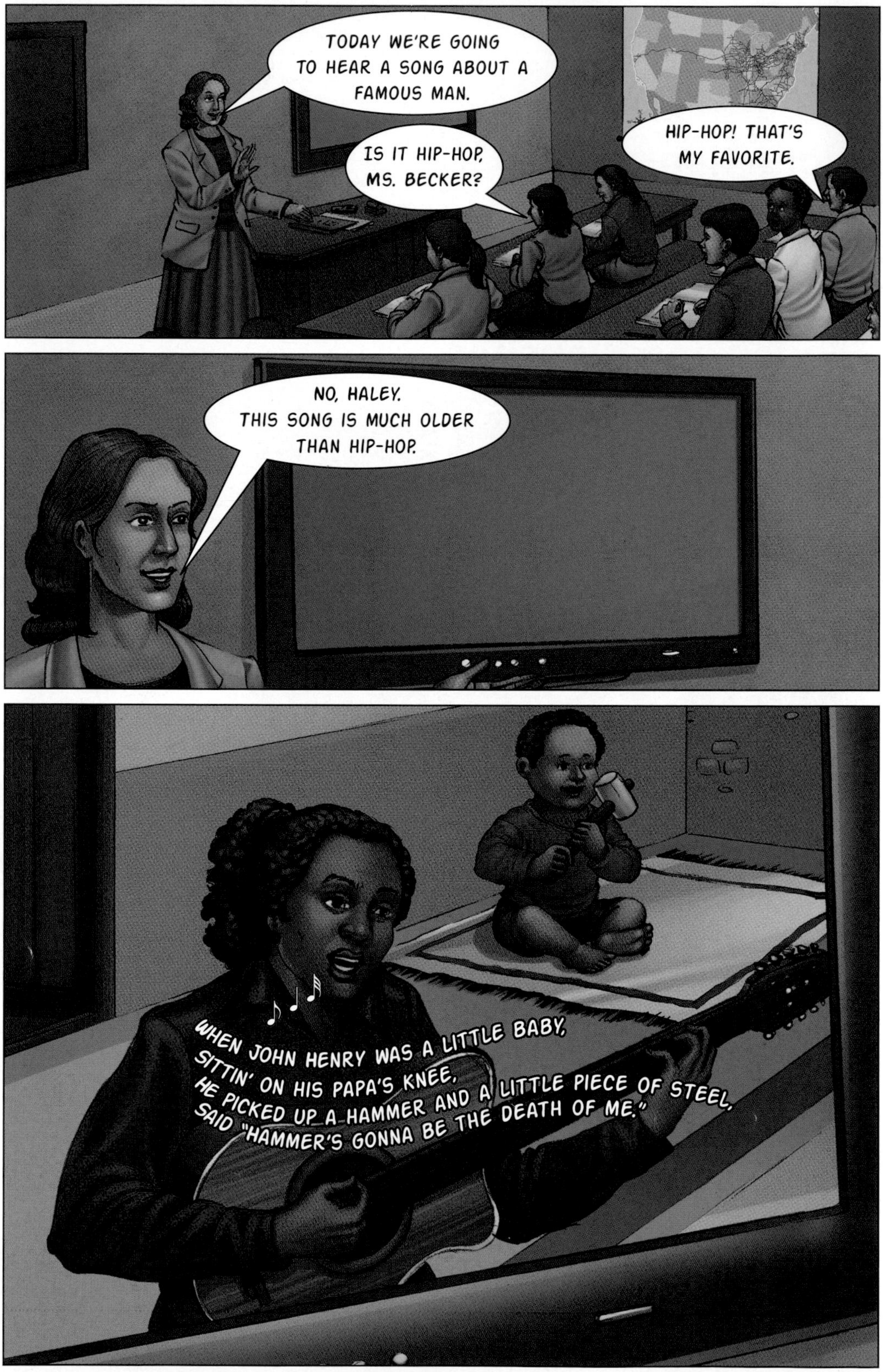
TODAY WE'RE GOING TO HEAR A SONG ABOUT A FAMOUS MAN.
IS IT HIP-HOP, MS. BECKER?
HIP-HOP! THAT'S MY FAVORITE.
NO, HALEY. THIS SONG IS MUCH OLDER THAN HIP-HOP.
WHEN JOHN HENRY WAS A LITTLE BABY,
SITTIN' ON HIS PAPA'S KNEE,
HE PICKED UP A HAMMER AND A LITTLE PIECE OF STEEL,
SAID "HAMMER'S GONNA BE THE DEATH OF ME."

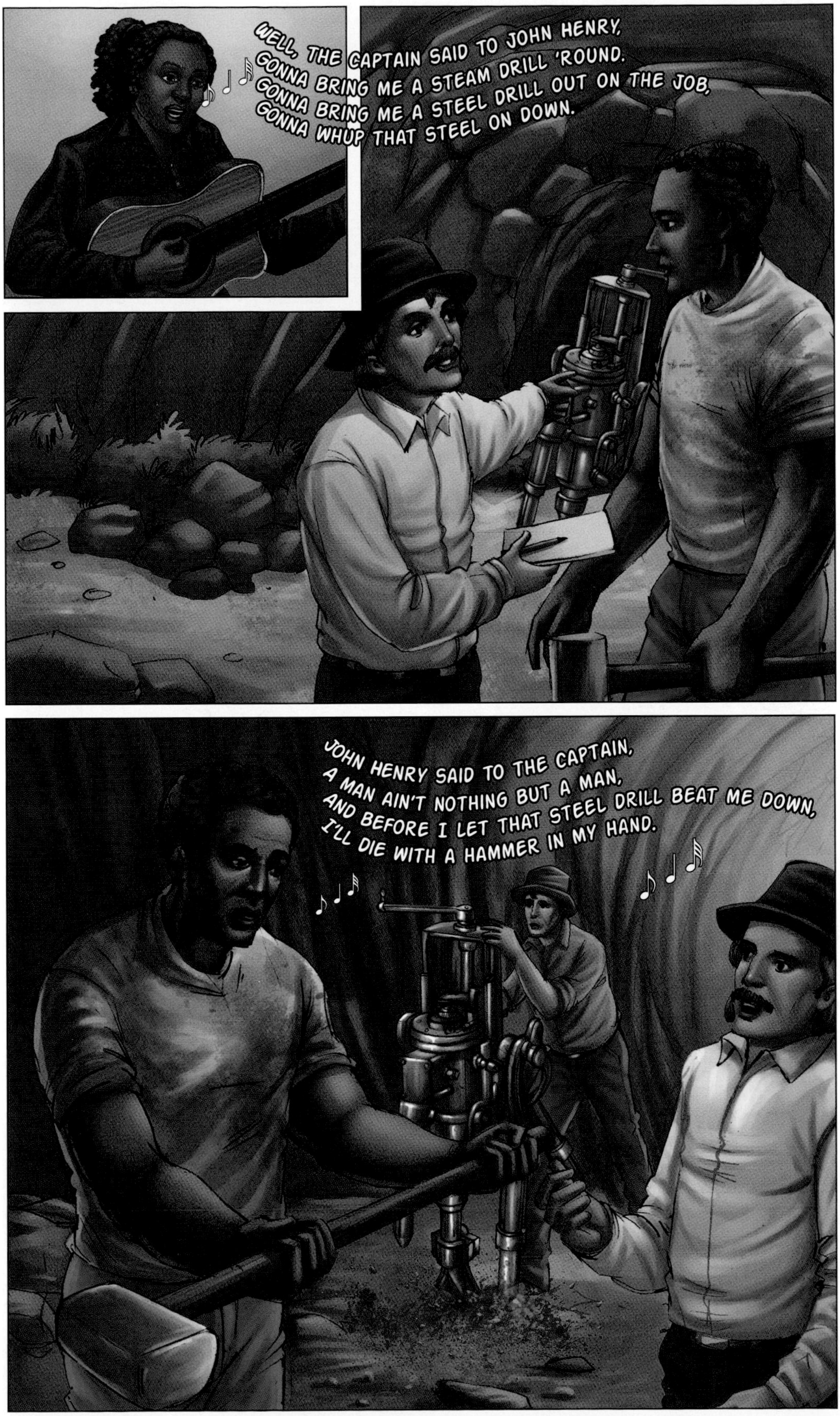
WELL, THE CAPTAIN SAID TO JOHN HENRY,
GONNA BRING ME A STEAM DRILL 'ROUND.
GONNA BRING ME A STEEL DRILL OUT ON THE JOB,
GONNA WHUP THAT STEEL ON DOWN.
JOHN HENRY SAID TO THE CAPTAIN,
A MAN AIN'T NOTHING BUT A MAN,
AND BEFORE I LET THAT STEEL DRILL BEAT ME DOWN,
I'LL DIE WITH A HAMMER IN MY HAND.

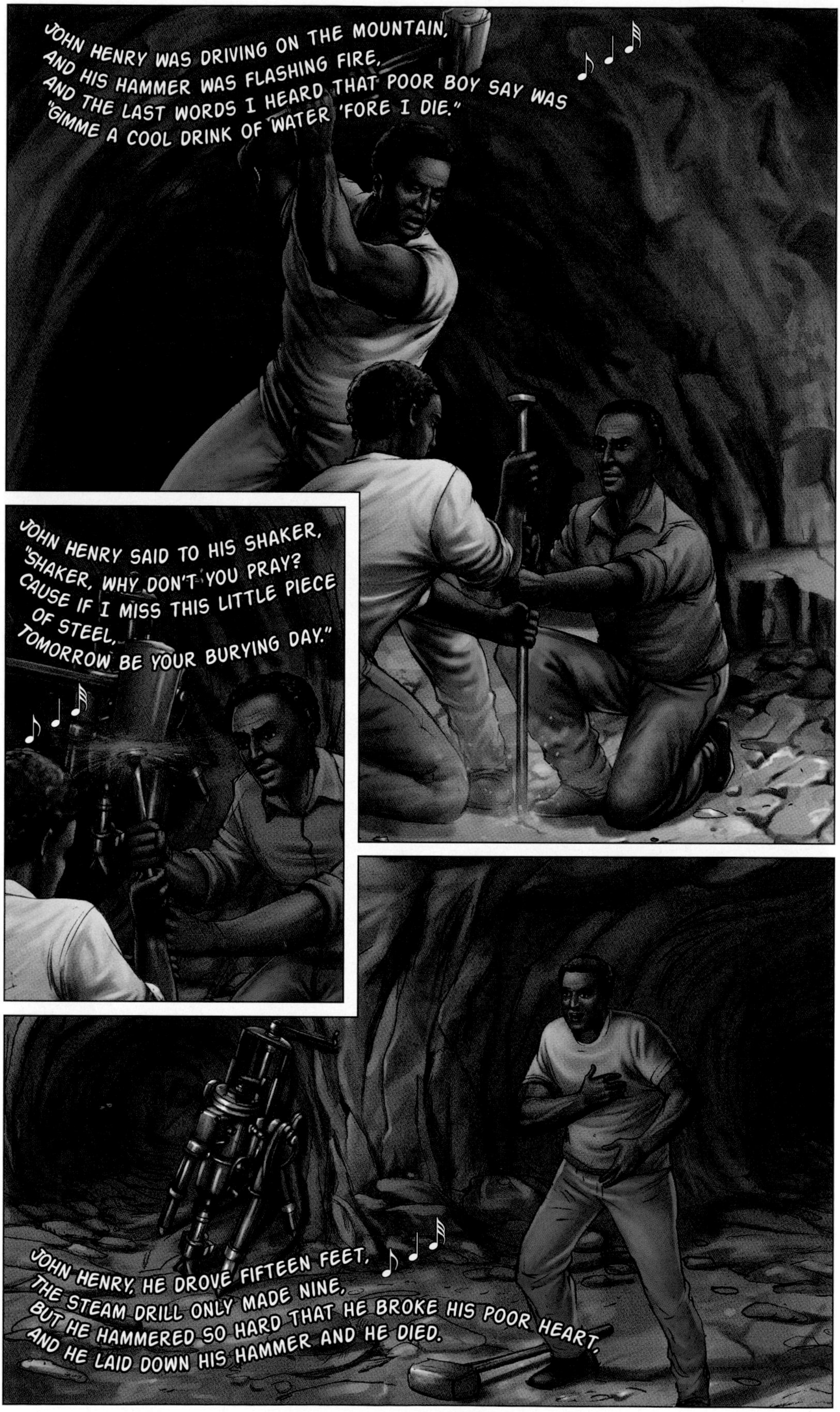
JOHN HENRY WAS DRIVING ON THE MOUNTAIN,
AND HIS HAMMER WAS FLASHING FIRE,
AND THE LAST WORDS I HEARD THAT POOR BOY SAY WAS
"GIMME A COOL DRINK OF WATER 'FORE I DIE."
JOHN HENRY SAID TO HIS SHAKER,
"SHAKER, WHY DON'T YOU PRAY?
CAUSE IF I MISS THIS LITTLE PIECE
OF STEEL,
TOMORROW BE YOUR BURYING DAY."
JOHN HENRY, HE DROVE FIFTEEN FEET,
THE STEAM DRILL ONLY MADE NINE,
BUT HE HAMMERED SO HARD THAT HE BROKE HIS POOR HEART,
AND HE LAID DOWN HIS HAMMER AND HE DIED.

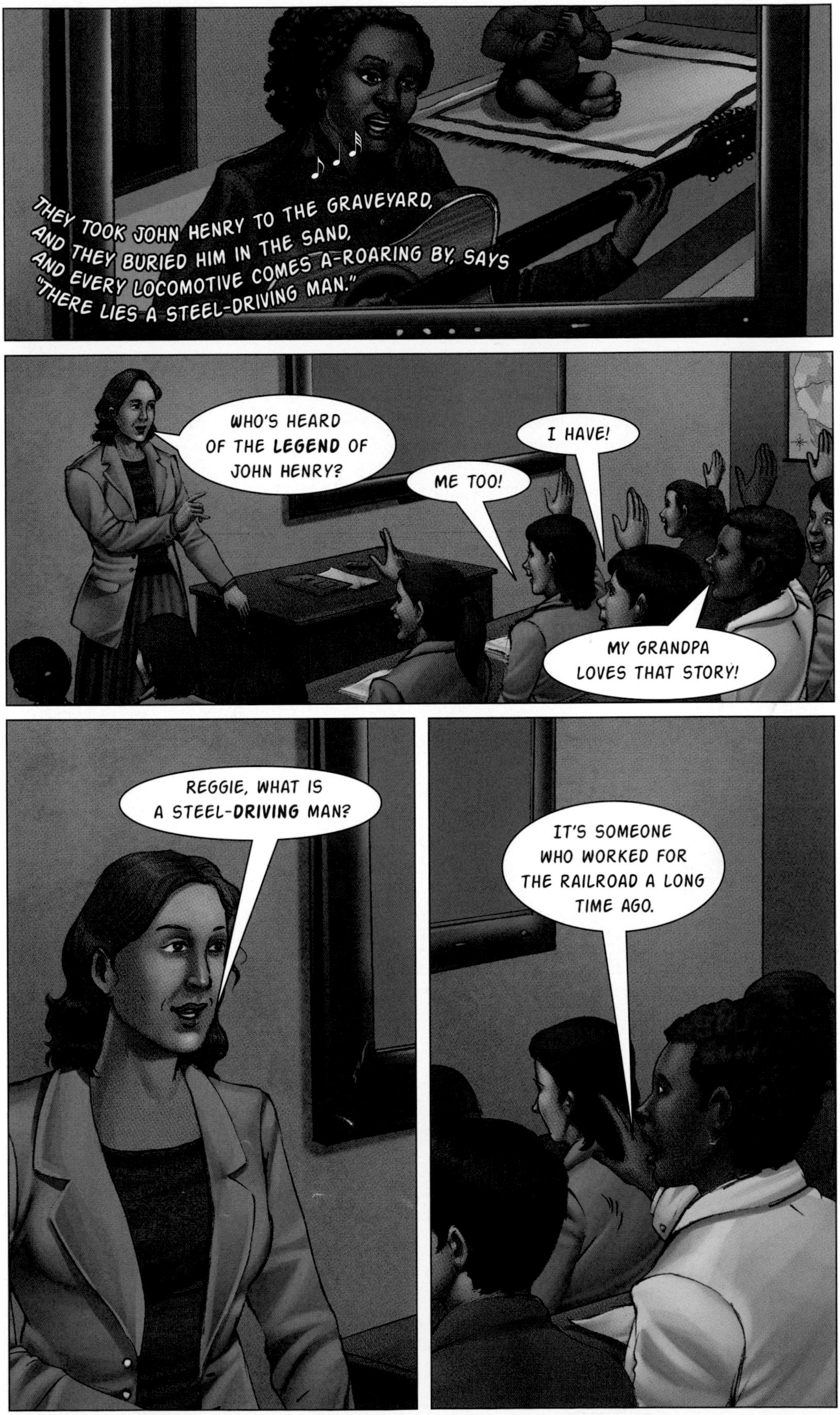

THEY TOOK JOHN HENRY TO THE GRAVEYARD,
AND THEY BURIED HIM IN THE SAND,
AND EVERY LOCOMOTIVE COMES A-ROARING BY, SAYS
"THERE LIES A STEEL-DRIVING MAN."
WHO'S HEARD OF THE **LEGEND** OF JOHN HENRY?
I HAVE!
ME TOO!
MY GRANDPA LOVES THAT STORY!
REGGIE, WHAT IS A STEEL-**DRIVING** MAN?
IT'S SOMEONE WHO WORKED FOR THE RAILROAD A LONG TIME AGO.

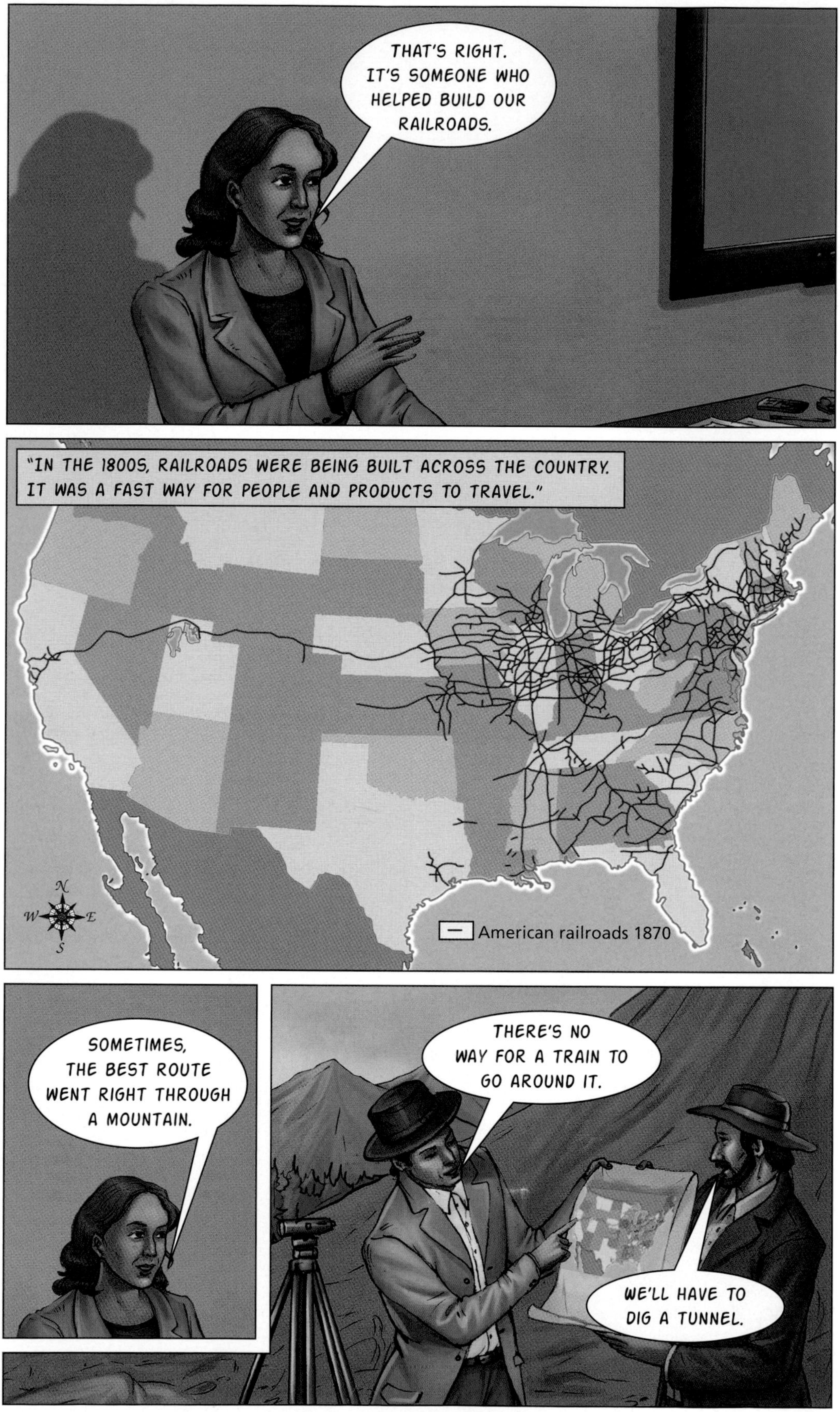
THAT'S RIGHT. IT'S SOMEONE WHO HELPED BUILD OUR RAILROADS.
"IN THE 1800S, RAILROADS WERE BEING BUILT ACROSS THE COUNTRY. IT WAS A FAST WAY FOR PEOPLE AND PRODUCTS TO TRAVEL."
N
W
E
S
American railroads 1870
SOMETIMES, THE BEST ROUTE WENT RIGHT THROUGH A MOUNTAIN.
THERE'S NO WAY FOR A TRAIN TO GO AROUND IT.
WE'LL HAVE TO DIG A TUNNEL.

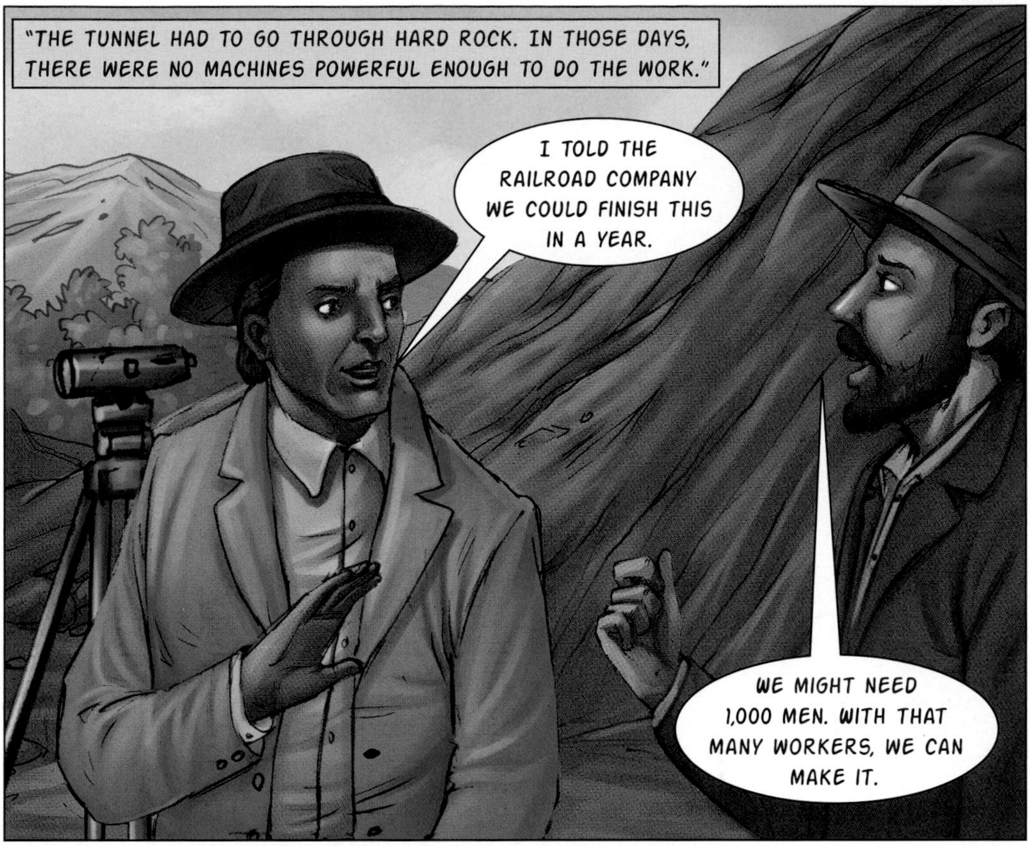
"THE TUNNEL HAD TO GO THROUGH HARD ROCK. IN THOSE DAYS, THERE WERE NO MACHINES POWERFUL ENOUGH TO DO THE WORK."
I TOLD THE RAILROAD COMPANY WE COULD FINISH THIS IN A YEAR.
WE MIGHT NEED 1,000 MEN. WITH THAT MANY WORKERS, WE CAN MAKE IT.

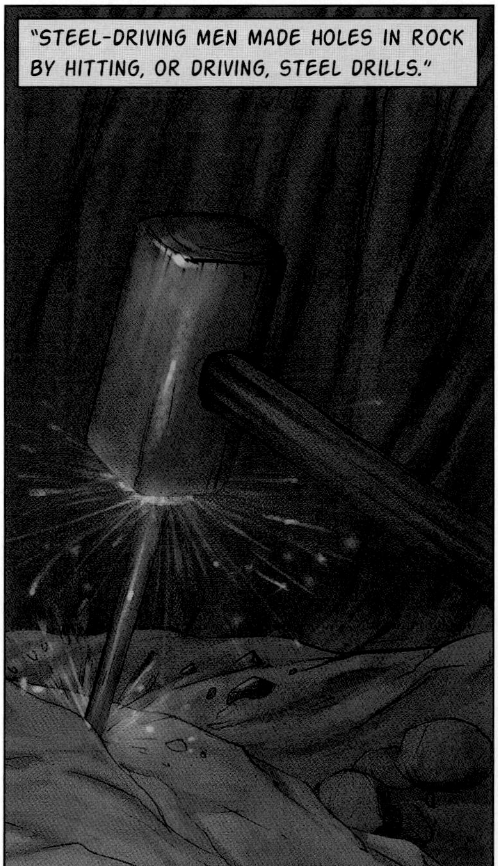
"STEEL-DRIVING MEN MADE HOLES IN ROCK BY HITTING, OR DRIVING, STEEL DRILLS."

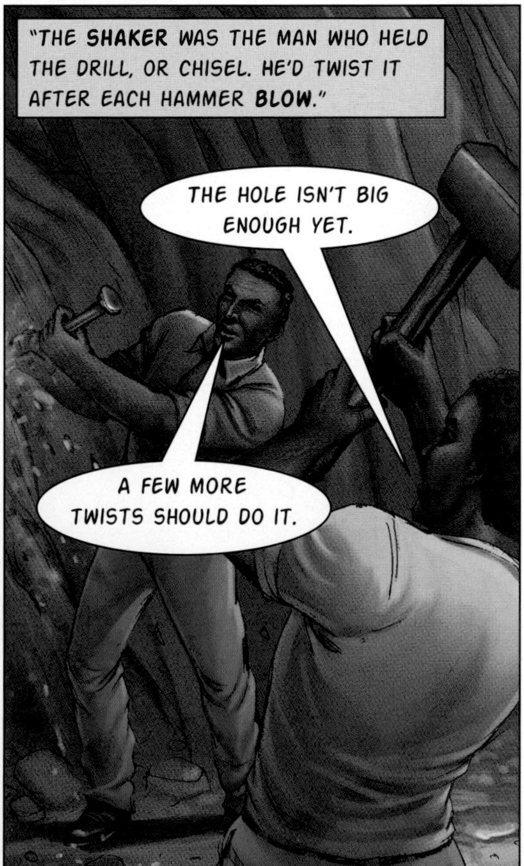
"THE SHAKER WAS THE MAN WHO HELD THE DRILL, OR CHISEL. HE'D TWIST IT AFTER EACH HAMMER BLOW."
THE HOLE ISN'T BIG ENOUGH YET.
A FEW MORE TWISTS SHOULD DO IT.

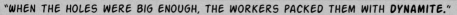
"WHEN THE HOLES WERE BIG ENOUGH, THE WORKERS PACKED THEM WITH **DYNAMITE**."

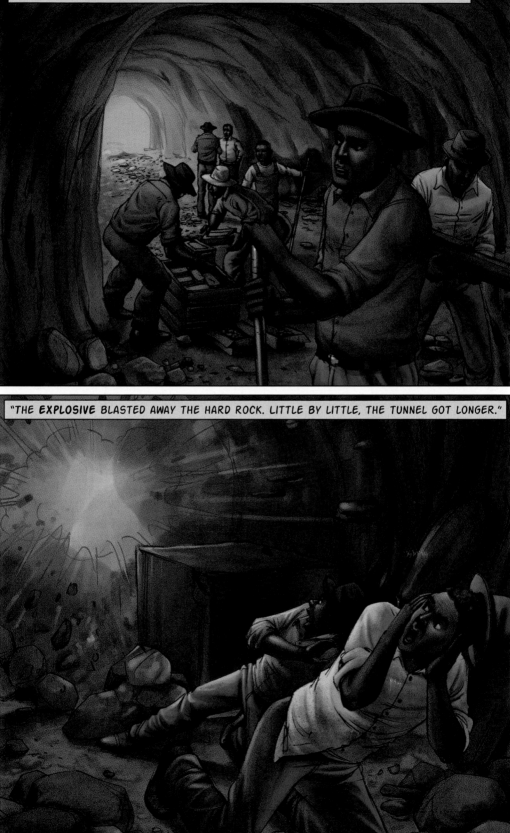
"THE **EXPLOSIVE** BLASTED AWAY THE HARD ROCK. LITTLE BY LITTLE, THE TUNNEL GOT LONGER."

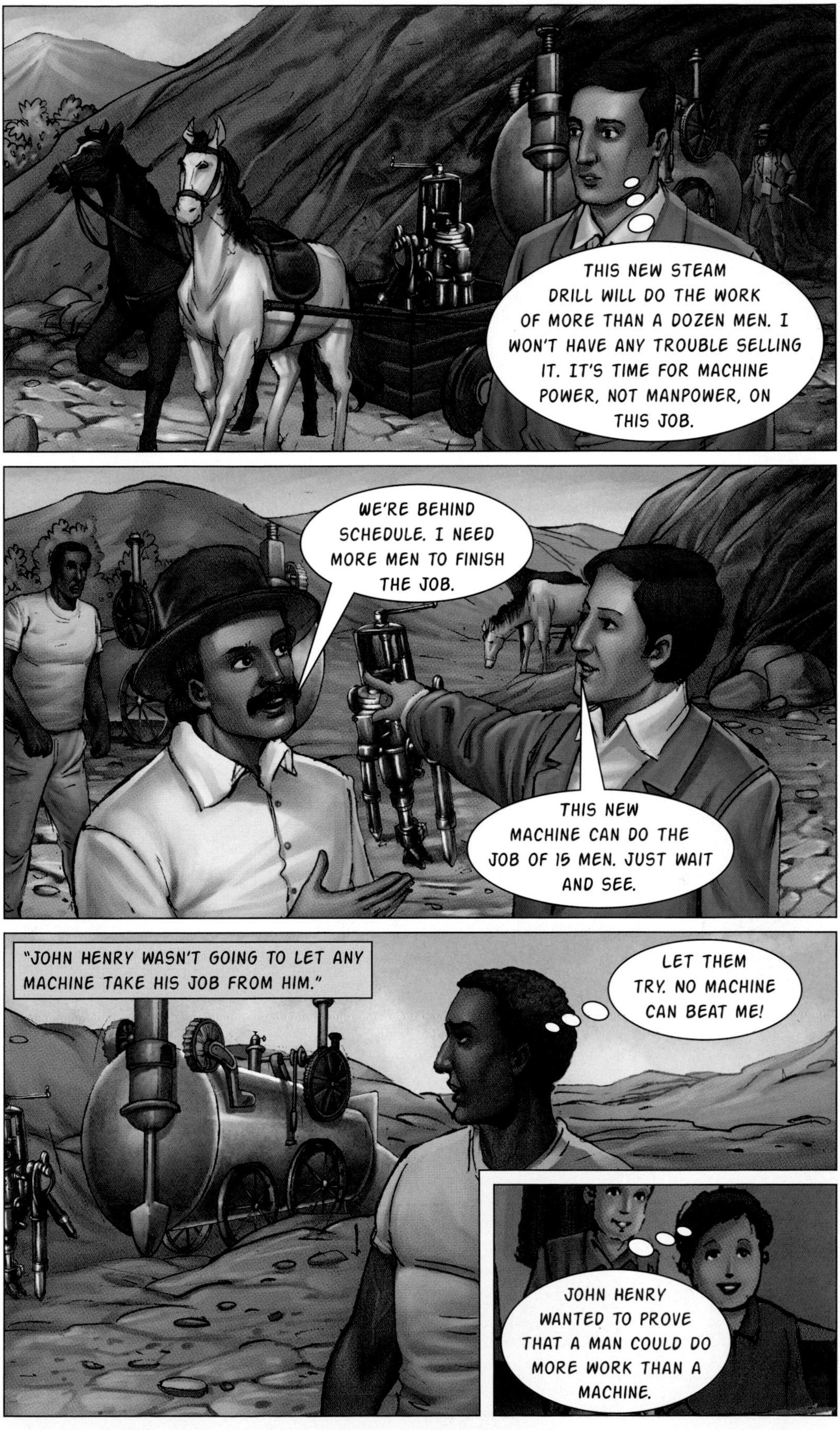
THIS NEW STEAM DRILL WILL DO THE WORK OF MORE THAN A DOZEN MEN. I WON'T HAVE ANY TROUBLE SELLING IT. IT'S TIME FOR MACHINE POWER, NOT MANPOWER, ON THIS JOB.
WE'RE BEHIND SCHEDULE. I NEED MORE MEN TO FINISH THE JOB.
THIS NEW MACHINE CAN DO THE JOB OF 15 MEN. JUST WAIT AND SEE.
"JOHN HENRY WASN'T GOING TO LET ANY MACHINE TAKE HIS JOB FROM HIM."
LET THEM TRY. NO MACHINE CAN BEAT ME!
JOHN HENRY WANTED TO PROVE THAT A MAN COULD DO MORE WORK THAN A MACHINE.

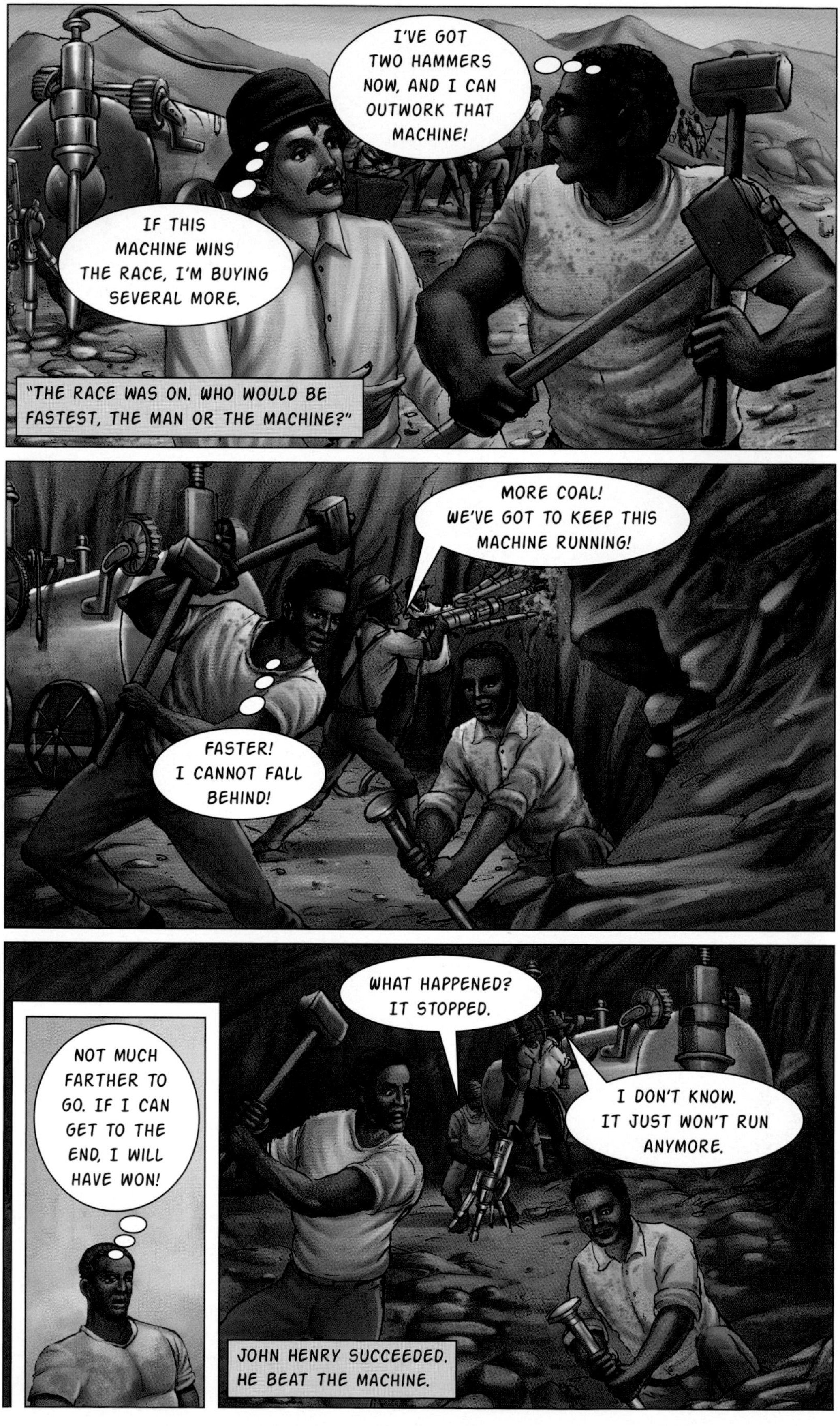
I'VE GOT TWO HAMMERS NOW, AND I CAN OUTWORK THAT MACHINE!
IF THIS MACHINE WINS THE RACE, I'M BUYING SEVERAL MORE.
"THE RACE WAS ON. WHO WOULD BE FASTEST, THE MAN OR THE MACHINE?"
MORE COAL! WE'VE GOT TO KEEP THIS MACHINE RUNNING!
FASTER! I CANNOT FALL BEHIND!
NOT MUCH FARTHER TO GO. IF I CAN GET TO THE END, I WILL HAVE WON!
WHAT HAPPENED? IT STOPPED.
I DON'T KNOW. IT JUST WON'T RUN ANYMORE.
JOHN HENRY SUCCEEDED. HE BEAT THE MACHINE.

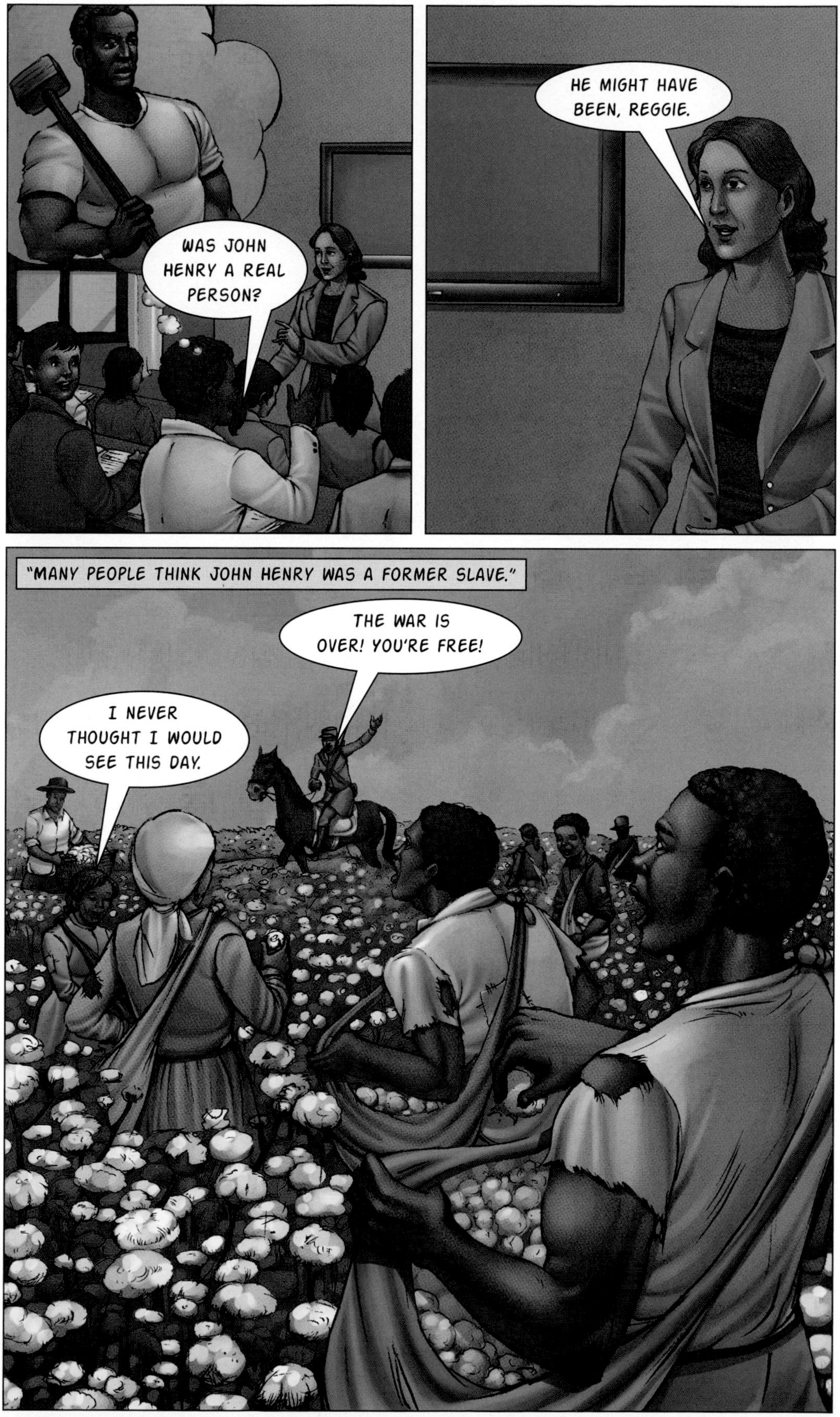
WAS JOHN HENRY A REAL PERSON?
HE MIGHT HAVE BEEN, REGGIE.
"MANY PEOPLE THINK JOHN HENRY WAS A FORMER SLAVE."
THE WAR IS OVER! YOU'RE FREE!
I NEVER THOUGHT I WOULD SEE THIS DAY.

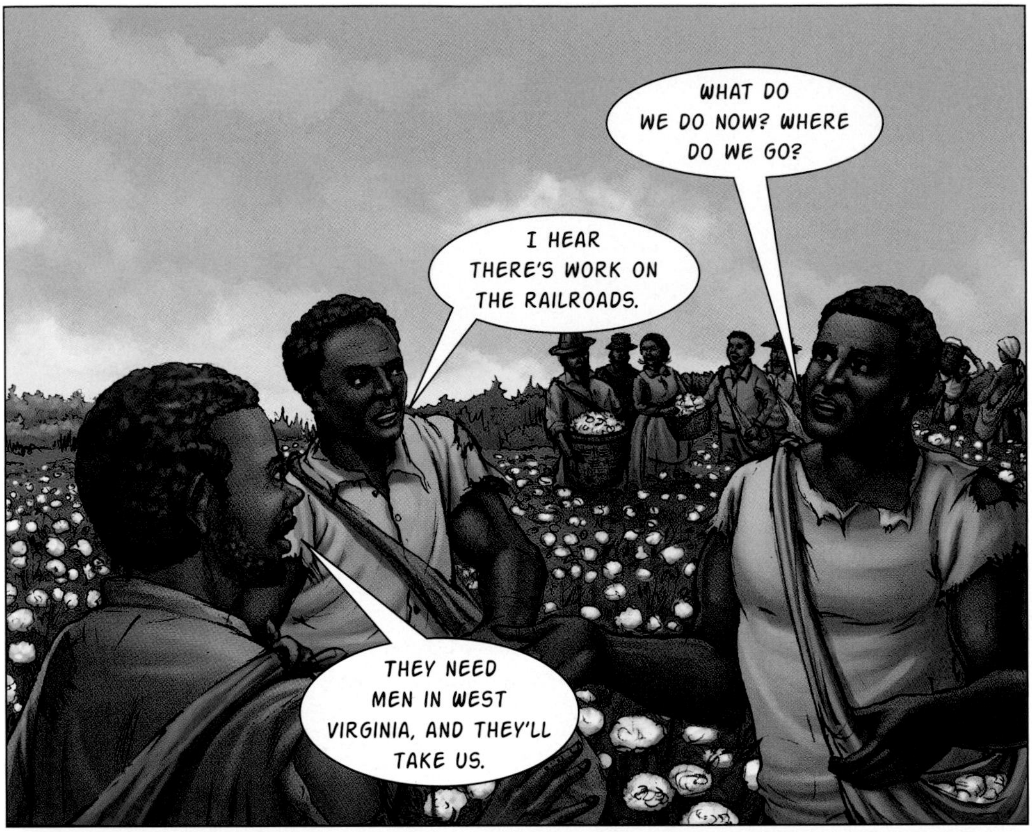
WHAT DO WE DO NOW? WHERE DO WE GO?
I HEAR THERE'S WORK ON THE RAILROADS.
THEY NEED MEN IN WEST VIRGINIA, AND THEY'LL TAKE US.

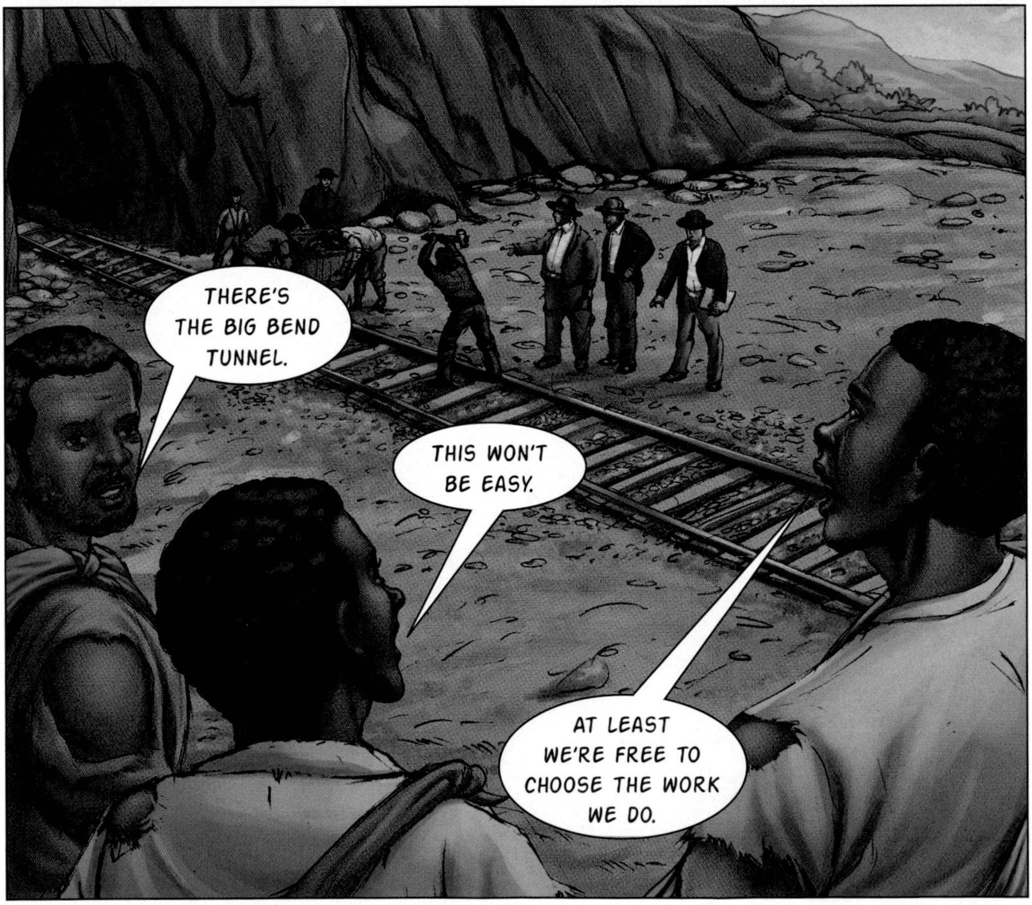
THERE'S THE BIG BEND TUNNEL.
THIS WON'T BE EASY.
AT LEAST WE'RE FREE TO CHOOSE THE WORK WE DO.

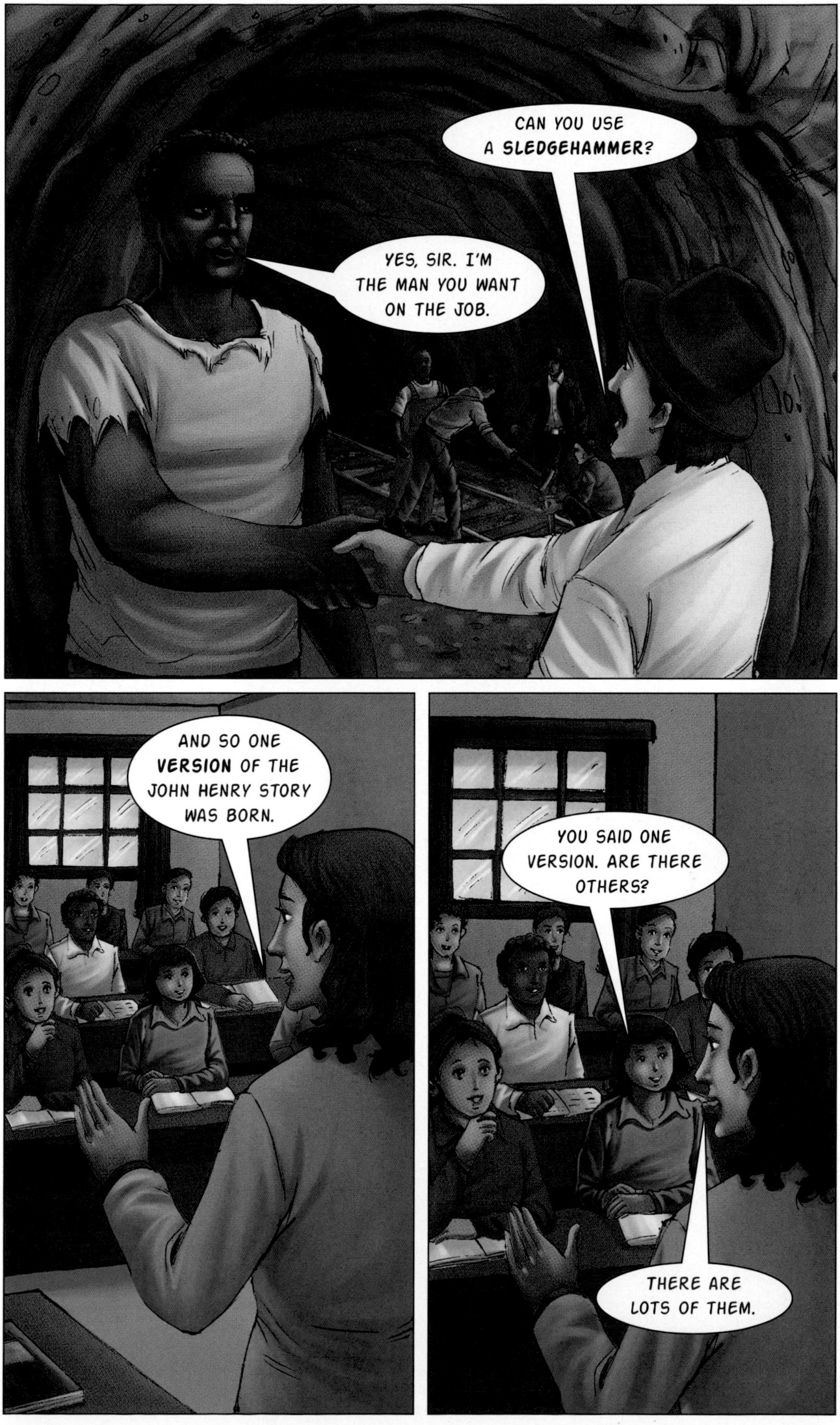
CAN YOU USE A **SLEDGEHAMMER**?
YES, SIR. I'M THE MAN YOU WANT ON THE JOB.
AND SO ONE **VERSION** OF THE JOHN HENRY STORY WAS BORN.
YOU SAID ONE VERSION. ARE THERE OTHERS?
THERE ARE LOTS OF THEM.

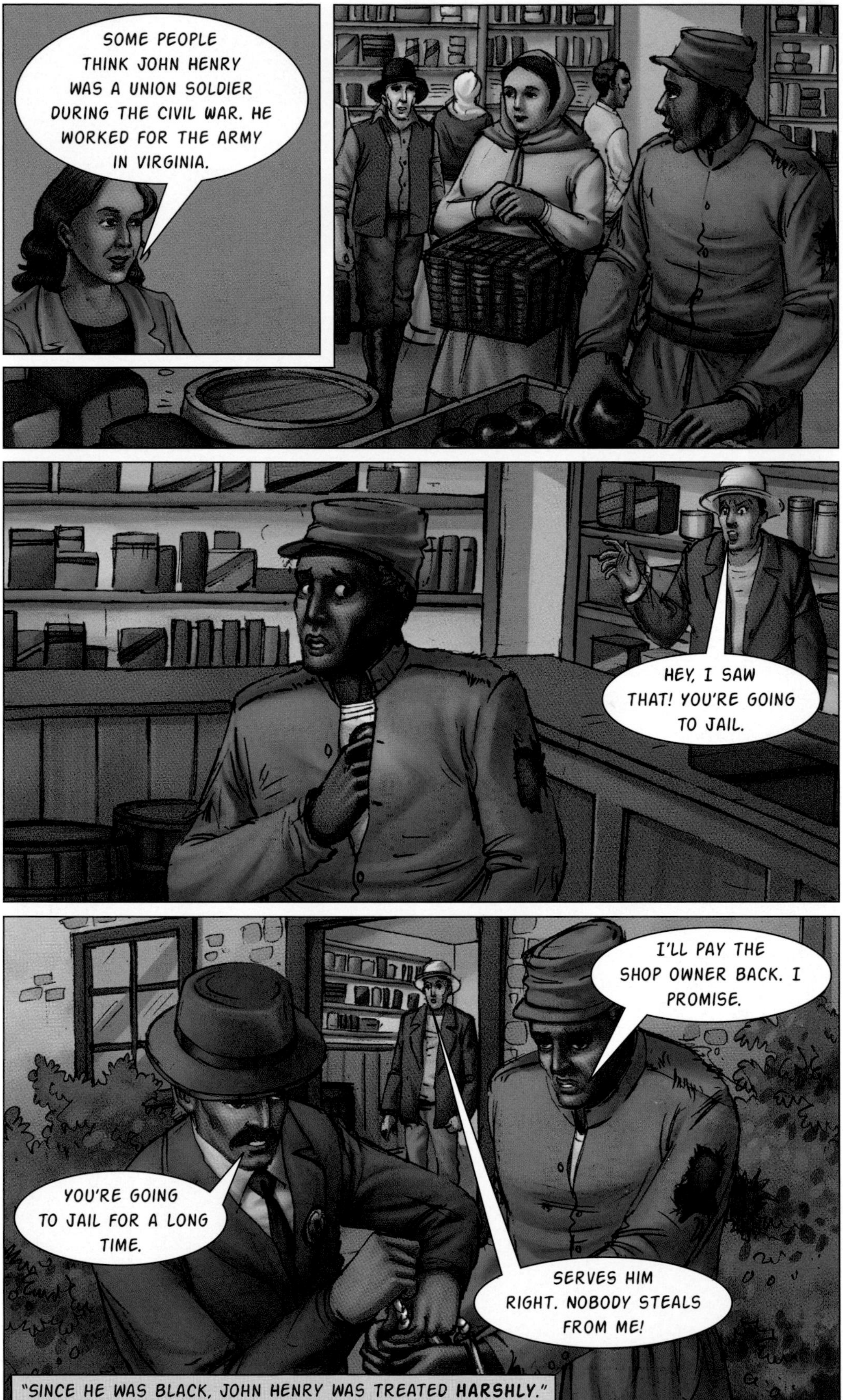
SOME PEOPLE THINK JOHN HENRY WAS A UNION SOLDIER DURING THE CIVIL WAR. HE WORKED FOR THE ARMY IN VIRGINIA.
HEY, I SAW THAT! YOU'RE GOING TO JAIL.
I'LL PAY THE SHOP OWNER BACK. I PROMISE.
YOU'RE GOING TO JAIL FOR A LONG TIME.
SERVES HIM RIGHT. NOBODY STEALS FROM ME!
"SINCE HE WAS BLACK, JOHN HENRY WAS TREATED HARSHLY."

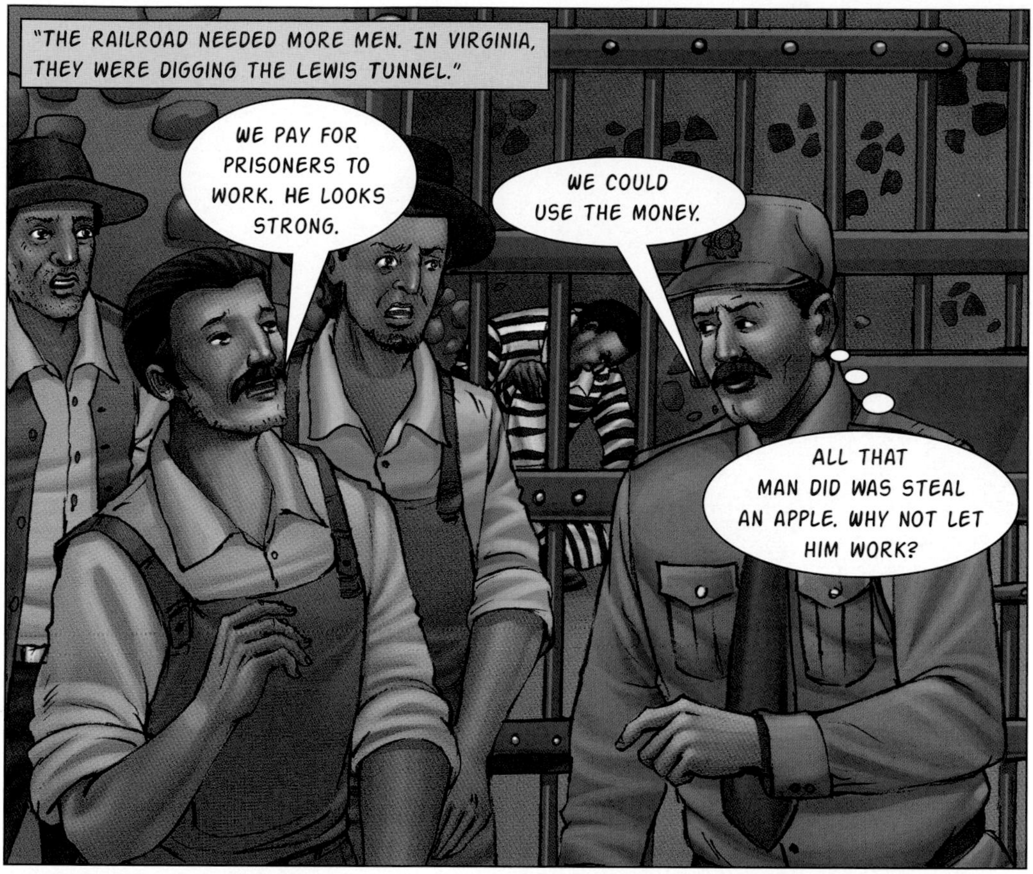
"THE RAILROAD NEEDED MORE MEN. IN VIRGINIA, THEY WERE DIGGING THE LEWIS TUNNEL."
WE PAY FOR PRISONERS TO WORK. HE LOOKS STRONG.
WE COULD USE THE MONEY.
ALL THAT MAN DID WAS STEAL AN APPLE. WHY NOT LET HIM WORK?

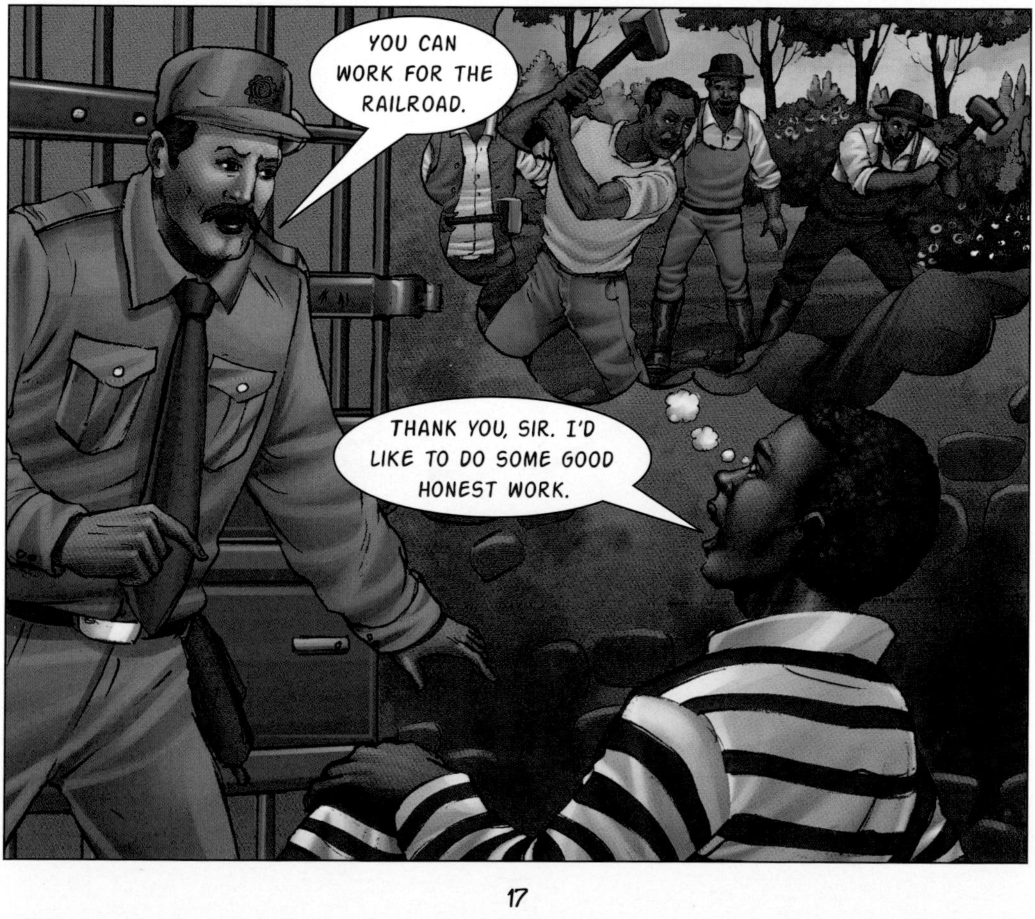
YOU CAN WORK FOR THE RAILROAD.
THANK YOU, SIR. I'D LIKE TO DO SOME GOOD HONEST WORK.

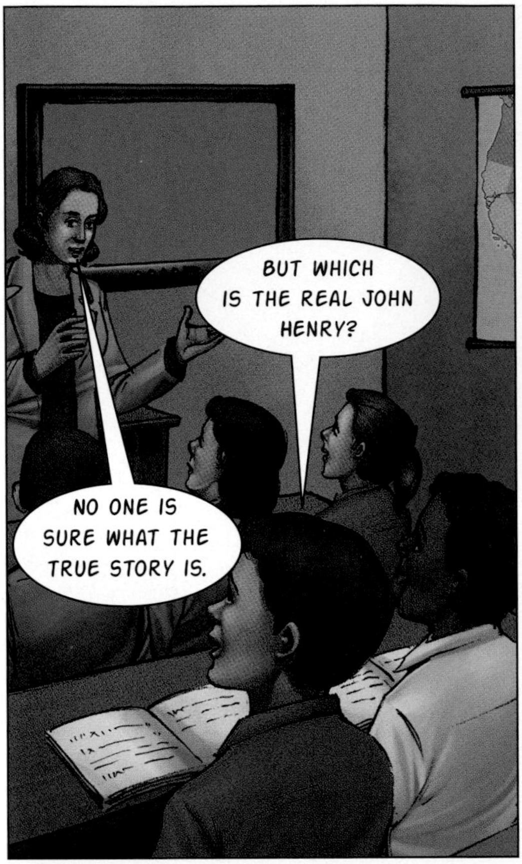
BUT WHICH IS THE REAL JOHN HENRY?
NO ONE IS SURE WHAT THE TRUE STORY IS.

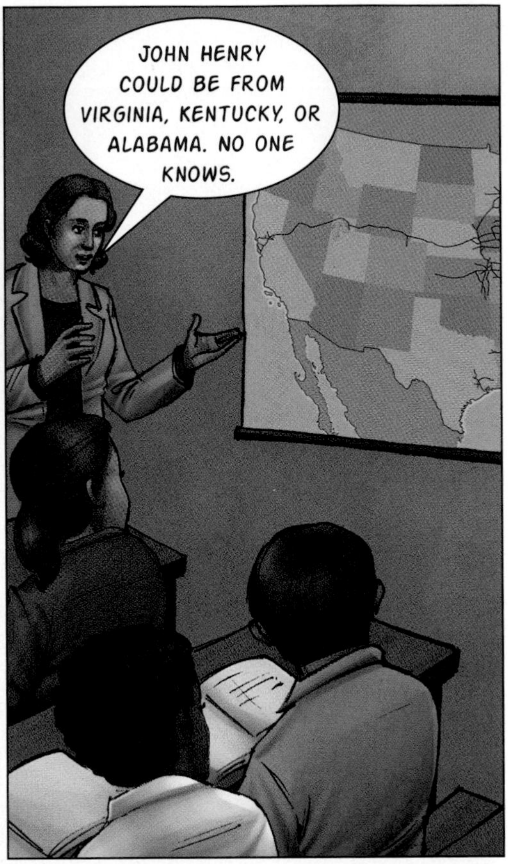
JOHN HENRY COULD BE FROM VIRGINIA, KENTUCKY, OR ALABAMA. NO ONE KNOWS.

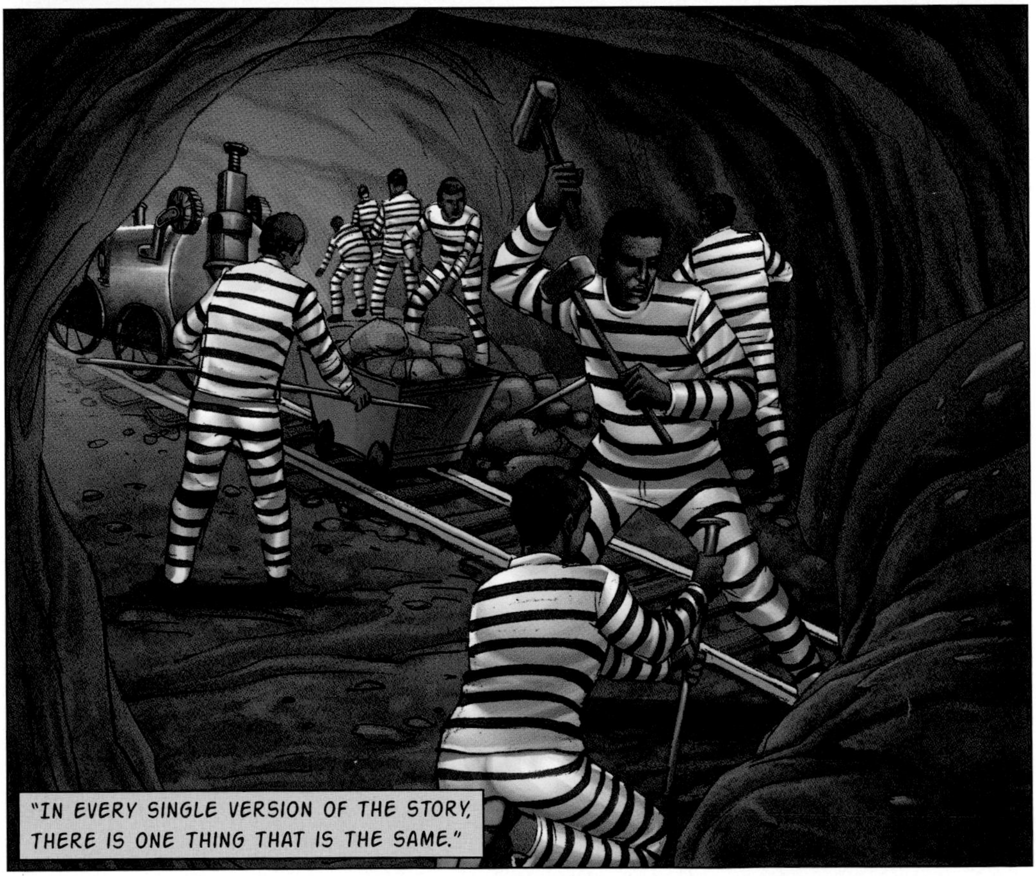
"IN EVERY SINGLE VERSION OF THE STORY, THERE IS ONE THING THAT IS THE SAME."

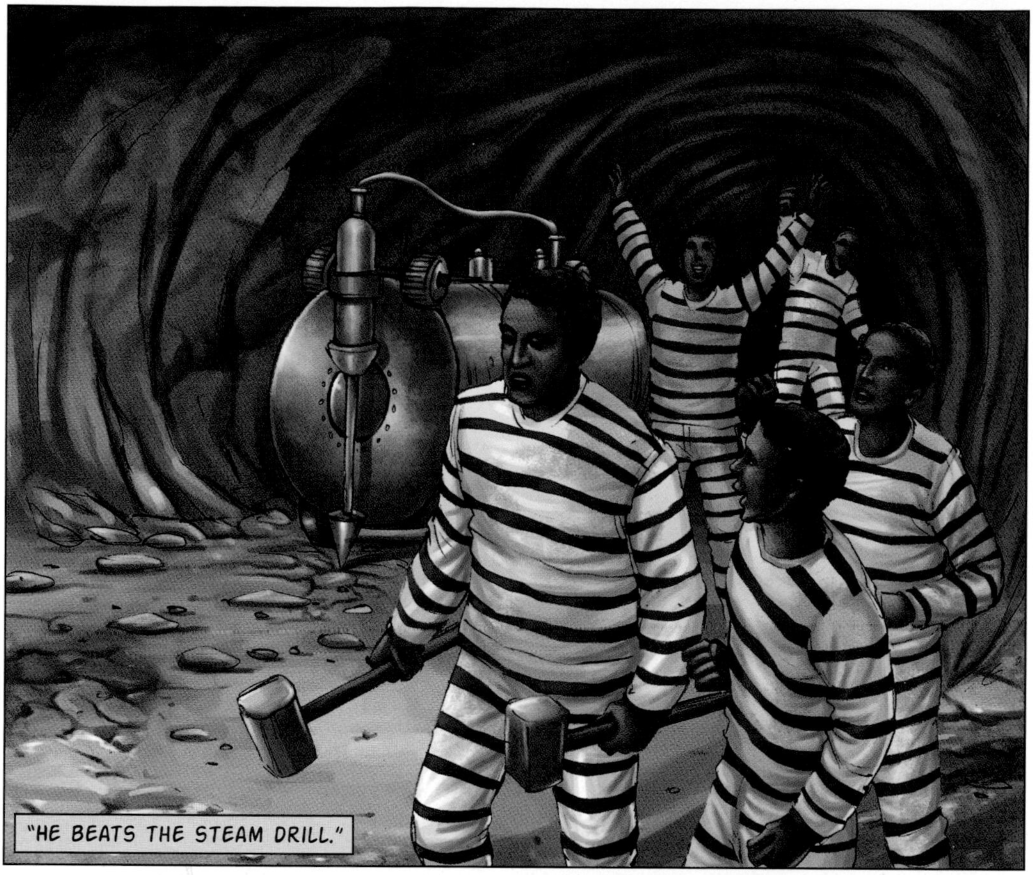
"HE BEATS THE STEAM DRILL."

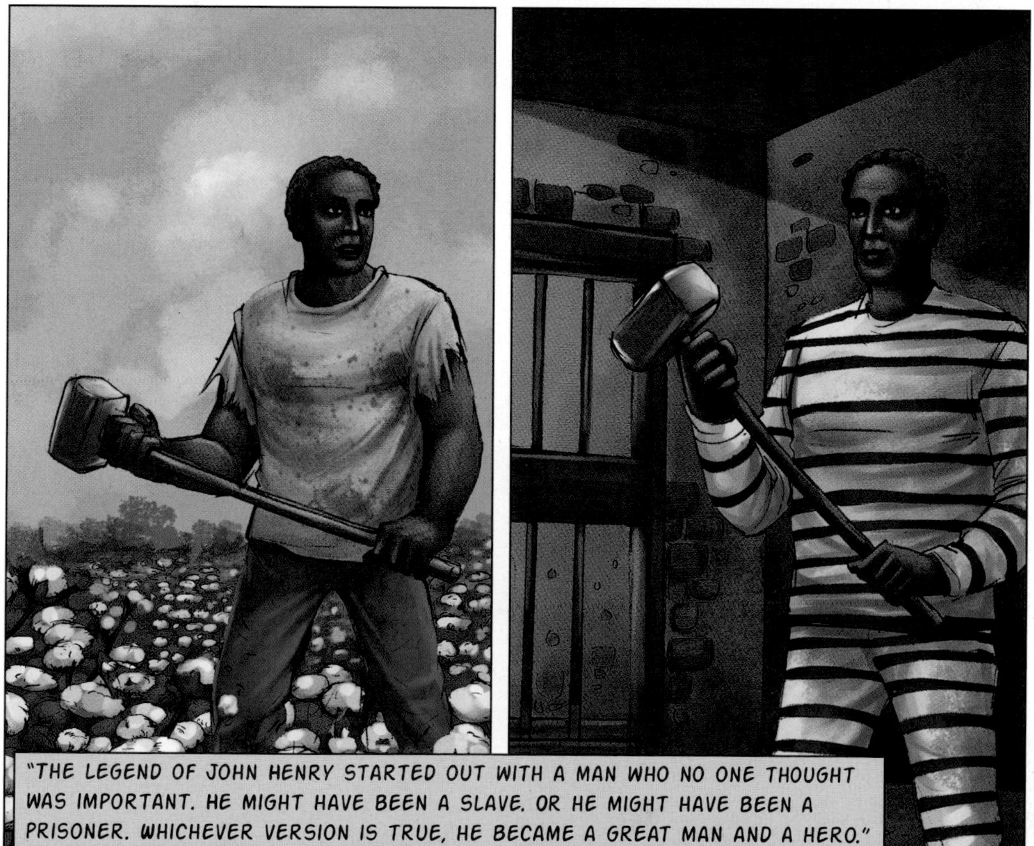
"THE LEGEND OF JOHN HENRY STARTED OUT WITH A MAN WHO NO ONE THOUGHT WAS IMPORTANT. HE MIGHT HAVE BEEN A SLAVE. OR HE MIGHT HAVE BEEN A PRISONER. WHICHEVER VERSION IS TRUE, HE BECAME A GREAT MAN AND A HERO."

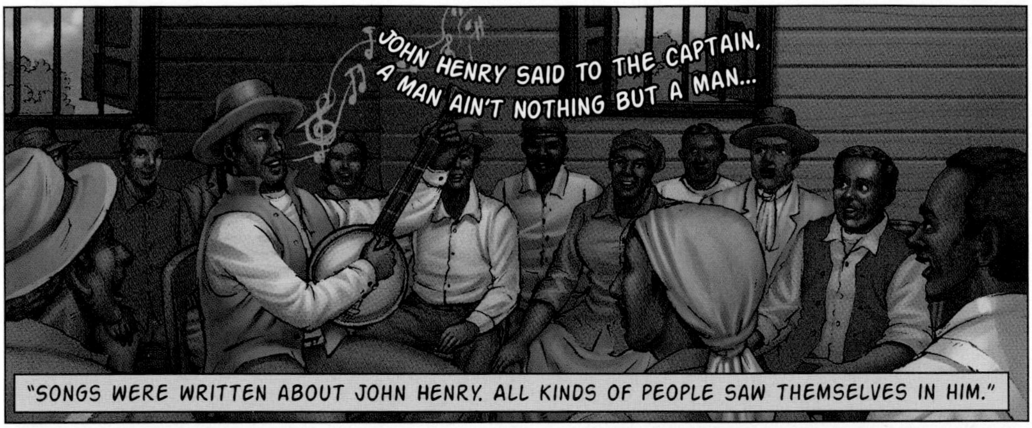
JOHN HENRY SAID TO THE CAPTAIN,
A MAN AIN'T NOTHING BUT A MAN...
"SONGS WERE WRITTEN ABOUT JOHN HENRY. ALL KINDS OF PEOPLE SAW THEMSELVES IN HIM."

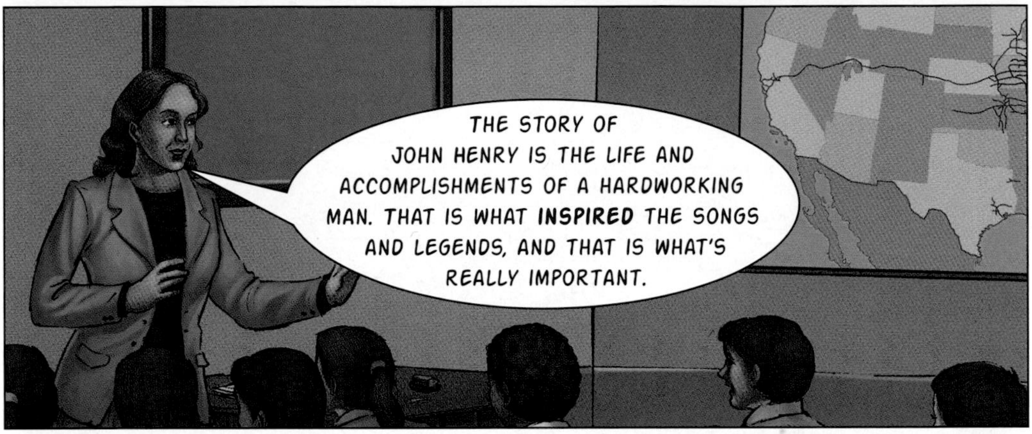
THE STORY OF JOHN HENRY IS THE LIFE AND ACCOMPLISHMENTS OF A HARDWORKING MAN. THAT IS WHAT INSPIRED THE SONGS AND LEGENDS, AND THAT IS WHAT'S REALLY IMPORTANT.

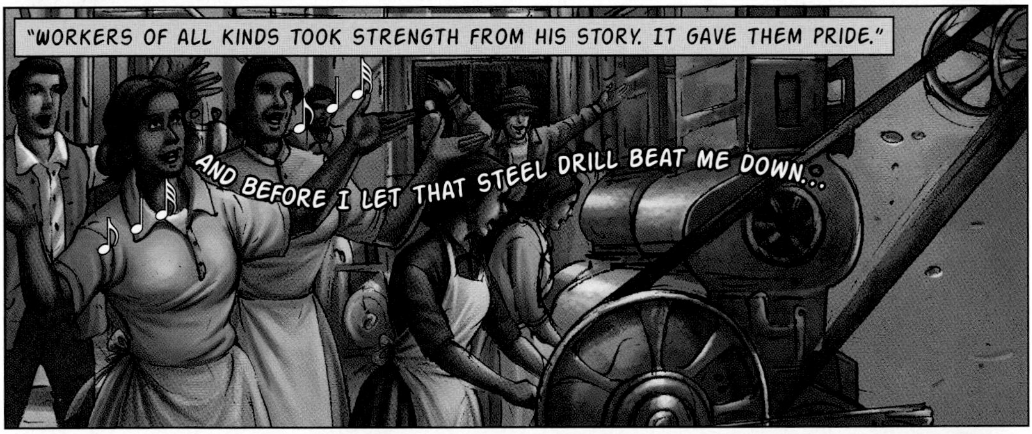
"WORKERS OF ALL KINDS TOOK STRENGTH FROM HIS STORY. IT GAVE THEM PRIDE."
AND BEFORE I LET THAT STEEL DRILL BEAT ME DOWN...

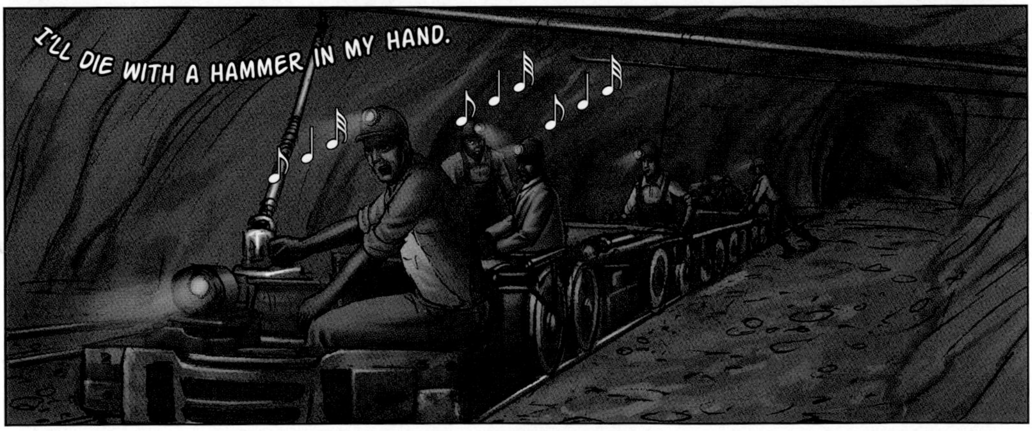
I'LL DIE WITH A HAMMER IN MY HAND.

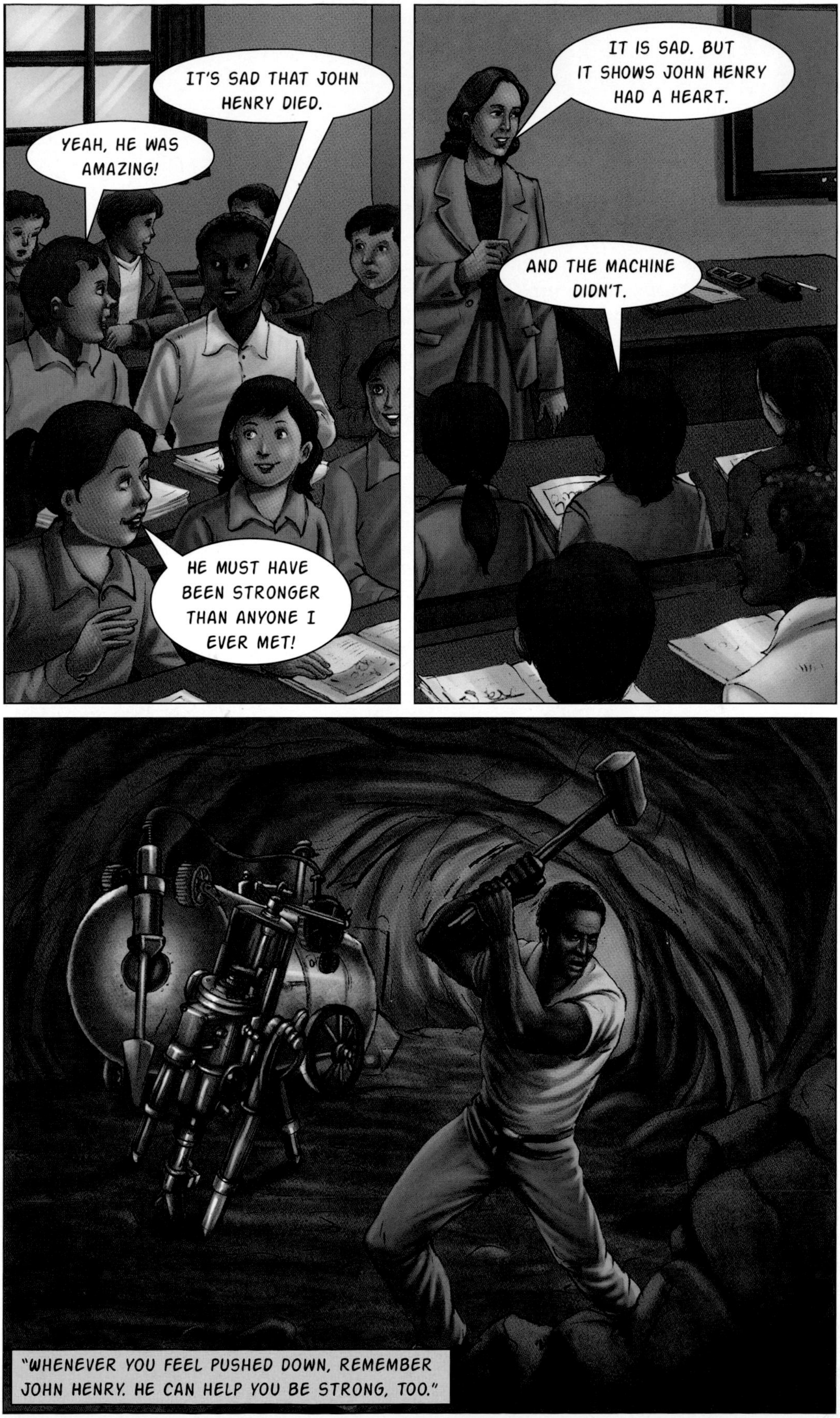
IT'S SAD THAT JOHN HENRY DIED.
YEAH, HE WAS AMAZING!
HE MUST HAVE BEEN STRONGER THAN ANYONE I EVER MET!
IT IS SAD. BUT IT SHOWS JOHN HENRY HAD A HEART.
AND THE MACHINE DIDN'T.
"WHENEVER YOU FEEL PUSHED DOWN, REMEMBER JOHN HENRY. HE CAN HELP YOU BE STRONG, TOO."

Timeline

1863–1869   The first railroad to cross the United States is built.

1865   The Civil War ends, and the slaves are freed.

c. 1868   According to one legend, John Henry was leased as a prison worker to the C&O (Chesapeake and Ohio) Railway. Later, he was assigned to help build the Big Bend Tunnel, in West Virginia. Other stories say it was the Lewis Tunnel, in Virginia. According to this version, John Henry died in 1873.

1870–1873   The Big Bend Tunnel is built. John Henry may have helped dig this tunnel.

1887   According to another legend, John Henry, an ex-slave, is hired by the C&W (Columbus and Western) Railway to help bore a tunnel through the Oak and Coosa Mountains, in Alabama.

1924   The first recording of a John Henry song is made.

1972   A statue of John Henry near the entrance to the Big Bend Tunnel, near Talcott, West Virginia, is completed.

2008   Leeds, Alabama, honors John Henry and his work on the Coosa Mountain Tunnel in its first Leeds Downtown Folk Festival and John Henry Celebration, which would become an annual celebration.

Glossary

blow (BLOH) Hitting something with great force.

Civil War (SIH-vul WOR) The war fought between the Northern and the Southern states of America from 1861 to 1865.

driving (DRYV-ing) Pushing through forcefully.

dynamite (DY-nuh-myt) A powerful explosive used in blasting rock.

explosive (ek-SPLOH-siv) Something that can blow up.

harshly (HAHRSH-lee) Roughly.

inspired (in-SPY-urd) Moved to create something.

legend (LEH-jend) A story, passed down through the years, that cannot be proved.

shaker (SHAY-ker) The man who held the chisel on a steel-driving team.

sledgehammer (SLEJ-ha-mer) A large, heavy hammer that must be used with both hands.

steam drill (STEEM DRIL) A steam-powered drill used to cut through rock.

version (VER-zhun) Something different from something else, or having a different form.

Index

WebSites

Due to the changing nature of Internet links, PowerKids Press has developed an online list of websites related to the subject of this book. This site is updated regularly. Please use this link to access the link:

www.powerkidslinks.com/jgam/henry/